BITCOIN INVESTING

Bitcoin and Cryptocurrency Investing

By Sam Sutton
~~~

BITCOIN

Mastering Bitcoin for Starters

By Sam Sutton

~~~

© Copyright 2018 By Sam Sutton
All Rights Reserved

The transmission, duplication or reproduction of any of the following work including specific information will be considered an illegal act irrespective of if it is done electronically or in print. This extends to creating a secondary or tertiary copy of the work or a recorded copy and is only allowed with express written consent from the Publisher. All additional right reserved.

The information in the following pages is broadly considered to be a truthful and accurate account of facts and as such any inattention, use or misuse of the information in question by the reader will render any resulting actions solely under their purview. There are no scenarios in which the publisher or the original author of this work can be in any fashion deemed liable for any hardship or damages that may befall them after undertaking information described herein. This book should not be taken as financial or investment advice, and the author does not take any responsibility for inaccuracies, omissions, or errors which may be found therein.

Additionally, the information in the following pages is intended only for informational purposes and should thus be thought of as universal. As befitting its nature, it is presented without assurance regarding its prolonged validity or interim quality. Trademarks that are mentioned are done without written consent and can in no way be considered an endorsement from the trademark holder.

The contents of this book are intended to convey general information only. You should not treat any information herein as a call to make any particular decision regarding cryptocurrency usage, legal matters, investments, taxes, cryptocurrency mining, exchange usage, wallet usage, etc. It is strongly suggested that you seek advice from your own financial, investment, tax, or legal adviser. This book should not be taken as financial or investment advice, and the author does not take any responsibility for inaccuracies, omissions, or errors. The author of this work is not responsible for any loss, damage, or inconvenience caused as a result of reliance on information as published on, or linked to, this book.

The author of this book has taken careful measures to share vital information about the subject. May its readers acquire the right knowledge, wisdom, inspiration, and succeed.

TABLE OF CONTENTS

Introduction 7

Chapter 1: What is Bitcoin? 9

Chapter 2: Getting Started with Bitcoin 17

Chapter 3: Understanding Blockchain and
Bitcoin Transactions 19

Chapter 4: Where to Keep Your Bitcoin 23

Chapter 5: Buying Bitcoin 27

Chapter 6: Using Bitcoin 31

Chapter 7: Investing in Bitcoin 33

Chapter 8: Bitcoin for Business 39

Chapter 9: Bitcoin mining 41

Chapter 10: Security of Bitcoin 45

Conclusion 47

INTRODUCTION

Congratulations on downloading this book and thank you for doing so.

The following chapters will teach you the ins and outs of investing in bitcoin and how you can turn it into a goldmine of profits:

Chapter 1 lays down the basics to help you to have a good understanding of what bitcoin really is.

Chapter 2 gives an overview and teaches how you can get started with using bitcoin.

Chapter 3 discusses the blockchain technology which is the backbone technology of bitcoin. It also explains how a bitcoin transaction works.

Chapter 4 talks about the different types of bitcoin wallets.

Chapter 5 teaches how you can buy bitcoins.

Chapter 6 is about using bitcoin. Learn about receiving, sending, and receiving bitcoins.

Chapter 7 teaches effective strategies that you can use to invest in bitcoin.

Chapter 8 talks about businesses that use bitcoins, as well as how *you* can easily use it for your own business.

Chapter 9 is about bitcoin mining. Learn about the different ways to mine bitcoins.

Chapter 10 talks about the security of using bitcoin.

There are plenty of books on this subject on the market, thanks again for choosing this one! Every effort was made to ensure it is full of as much useful information as possible. Please enjoy!

CHAPTER 1:
WHAT IS BITCOIN?

Bitcoin is undeniably the number one cryptocurrency in the world. What is a *cryptocurrency*? A cryptocurrency is a kind of digital asset that is held electronically. It is stored online; and therefore, it does not have a physical existence. Just like other cryptocurrencies, bitcoin functions as a substitute for money.

Bitcoin is a *decentralized* digital currency. It is decentralized in the sense that there is no government, organization, group, or person that exercises authority over it. This makes it free from any and all forms of manipulation and undue advantage. This is also why so many people trust bitcoin.

It should be noted that although cryptocurrencies like bitcoin work as a substitute for money, they are not considered as fiat money or legal tender. Fiat money refers to the established and official currency of a state such as the US dollar. Legal tender refers to "that which a debtor may compel a creditor to accept payment." Although bitcoin is not considered as fiat money or legal tender, it is noteworthy that many individuals and merchants these days now accept bitcoin as a medium of payment. In fact, among all the cryptocurrencies out there, bitcoin is the most accepted cryptocurrency. Just to give you an idea, the giant computer company, Microsoft, now accepts payments in bitcoins. Not only that, Virgin Galactic, a huge company engaged in space tourism, also accepts payments in bitcoins. Other known companies like Overstock, Fiverr, Steam, Peach Airlines, Lionsgate Films, and Stripe, among many others, accept and use bitcoins. As Bitcoin gets more and more popular in the market, the more people and businesses start to use it.

Brief History

In 2008, a paper was posted on a cryptography mailing list. It was entitled *Bitcoin: A Peer-to-Peer Electronic Cash System*. It was published under the name Satoshi Nakamoto, which turned out to be just a pseudonym. The following year, Bitcoin was finally launched in the market. It came into existence just after Nakamoto himself mined the very first bitcoin block known as the *genesis block*.

Back then, bitcoin did not have any significant value. In fact, so many people did not even realize how much bitcoin would grow. At that time, it was the members of the cryptocurrency community themselves who decided how much bitcoin would worth. For example, there was a famous transaction where two pizzas where bought for 10,000 bitcoins. This is still posted on the *bitcointalk* forum. As you can see, most of the people there did not take it seriously. If only they knew how much bitcoin would develop. As of January 16, 2018, the price of 1 bitcoin is around 13,500 USD.

Who is Satoshi Nakamoto?

When people talk about the creator of bitcoin, they are well aware that it was made by Satoshi Nakamoto. But, who exactly is Satoshi Nakamoto? The truth is that up to the present time, nobody knows the real identity of Satoshi Nakamoto. There are many different views about this: There are those who say that Nakamoto is actually composed of a group of computer experts and programmers, while others say that Nakamoto is even a woman. Another theory is that Satoshi Nakamoto is Hal Finney, the man who first downloaded the bitcoin software and received 10 bitcoins from Nakamoto simply for downloading it. However, when Mr. Finney was still alive, he had already denied this claim. It is also worth mentioning that *Satoshi* is also the smallest unit of bitcoin. Bitcoin has 8 decimal places. Example: $0.00000001 = 1$ satoshi. Simply put, no one knows for certain the true identity of Satoshi Nakamoto. Nakamoto has long withdrawn from the public that nobody even knows his whereabouts. However, even though nobody knows who the real Satoshi Nakamoto is, and even if his identity remains a mystery forever, the fruit of his labor and contribution to the world, bitcoin, has gained worldwide popularity and success.

Why Invest in Bitcoin?

It is not a secret that most people who engage in the cryptocurrency market and possess bitcoins do not really use such cryptocurrency as a mere medium of exchange. In fact, they view bitcoin as a form of investment. So, you must be thinking: *Just how much profit can I reasonably make?* To give you an idea, here is the classic example: If you had invested even just $500 in bitcoin in 2009 or even in 2010, then you would have already earned millions by now. Yes, this is how profitable investing in bitcoin can be. Unlike investing in stocks where an annual return of 30% is already considered very high, you can obviously earn so much more when you invest in bitcoin. Hence, many professional stock investors have started moving their investments from stocks into bitcoins. Another benefit of investing in bitcoin is that you do not have to wait for a year just to experience a significant price increase. It is not uncommon for the price of bitcoin to increase by more than 30% within a week. There was even a time when the price of bitcoin increased by $2,000 in just a week's time.

Investing in bitcoin is also easy and convenient. Since cryptocurrencies are held electronically online, all you need is Internet access to start investing, and you can manage your account and all your investments in the comfort of your home. In fact, you can even do all these directly from your mobile phone. Indeed, now is the time for you to enjoy the beauty of technology and the profitability of bitcoin.

Of course, just like any other investment, there is also a risk that you may not earn anything and that you may even lose your investment. However, there are strategies that you can do to prevent this from happening. By using the right strategies as revealed in this book, you can effectively increase your rate of success by more than 75%.

So, should you invest in bitcoin? Well, if you are the type who is afraid of taking risks, then perhaps this investment is not right for you. However, if you are the type who wants to earn and enjoy a high amount of profit, if you are willing to take risks and spend time and effort to study the market, if you want a proven way to achieve financial freedom, then investing in bitcoin might just be the best investment decision that you can ever make.

High Volatility

When people talk about bitcoin, they usually say that it has a high volatility. This is true. But, what does it mean when you say that bitcoin has a *high volatility*? This means that the price of bitcoin changes rapidly and significantly. This explains why it is possible for you to earn more than 200% profit in just a few days. However, be careful about this since this also implies that it is also possible for the price of bitcoin to drop just as fast. This is a normal part of the risk of investing in bitcoin or any other cryptocurrency. The whole cryptocurrency market itself is simply highly volatile. However, do not let this discourage you. Just remember that it is exactly this high volatility nature of bitcoin that makes it a highly lucrative investment. The good news is that if you study the past and current trend of bitcoin, you can easily see that it is a very profitable investment. Indeed, the price of bitcoin as of the beginning of 2018 has been gradually decreasing. However, keep in mind that it first increased significantly. This is merely part of the usual fluctuations that you can expect in the market. The important thing is that, in the long run, the value of your investment should be growing. Bitcoin has well established itself for years, and nobody can deny that it is still the number one and most successful cryptocurrency in the market.

Be careful with your understanding of high volatility. Many people think that high volatility means that after a significant price increase, then the price will drop significantly afterward, and vice versa, as if it balancing the rise and fall of the price on its own. This is a wrong understanding of high volatility. Take note that bitcoin (as well as other cryptocurrencies) does not balance itself on its own. Instead, some factors affect its price, such as market competition, economy, technological developments, market acceptance, and government regulations, among many others. Hence, you need to consider all these factors when predicting whether the price of bitcoin will rise or fall, but rest assured that a cryptocurrency will not balance its price movements all by itself. This is also why you need to do research and analysis when you engage in the cryptocurrency market.

What are Altcoins?

When you read about bitcoin, you will definitely also encounter other cryptocurrencies like Ethereum, Litecoin, Ripple, Lisk, OmiseGO, and others. All of these are altcoins. Simply put, all cryptocurrencies are considered as altcoin except bitcoin. Bitcoin has established itself strongly in the market that it has become the leading standard of all cryptocurrencies, such that all other coins are merely called as *altcoins*, a term that is simply short for *alternative coins*. To date, there are already more than 1,000 altcoins that have been created. Still, among all the cryptocurrencies in the world, Bitcoin holds the number one position and is considered the top and most successful and popular cryptocurrency of all.

Anonymity

Bitcoin users enjoy a certain level of anonymity. This is because, in a bitcoin transaction, no personal details will be revealed. This is true even though bitcoin has a *public* blockchain. When you look at the bitcoin blockchain, you will only see a bitcoin wallet address of the sender and of the bitcoin wallet address of the recipient. You will also see the amount of bitcoins involved in the transaction, as well as a time stamp. However, the names and other sensitive information will remain confidential. What about the bitcoin wallet address? It is simply like a long string of random letters and numbers, and a bitcoin user can always request for a new wallet address for free with just a few clicks of a mouse. In fact, it is suggested that to minimize exposure, you should request for a new wallet address for every new transaction that you make.

On legal matters

Although bitcoin is decentralized in such a way that no central authority governs and controls it, it does not mean that states do not have the power to regulate its use within their jurisdiction. Due to the level of anonymity enjoyed by bitcoin users, it is not hard to understand why some states like Ecuador and Bolivia completely outlaw the use of bitcoins, as well as all other cryptocurrencies. Due to the nature of cryptocurrencies, they can easily be used in illegal activities like money laundering and tax evasion. The good news is that in many countries like in the U.S., Canada, Europe, Russia, South Korea, Singapore, Philippines, and so many others, the use of bitcoins and other cryptocurrencies is legal. Russia used to consider it as illegal but then it changed its position in 2017 and now also uses bitcoin. Over time, more and more states and businesses are being open to the use of bitcoin.

As a bitcoin investor, you should keep an eye on the latest government regulations on bitcoin and other cryptocurrencies. Although there are states that do not outlaw the use of bitcoin in their territories, it does not mean that they can no longer impose regulations on the use of bitcoin. As of recently, the price of bitcoin and other known cryptocurrencies have been experiencing a decline. According to the news, this is because of certain regulations imposed by various states. But, do not worry; this has always been expected to happen. This is just one of the fluctuations that you can expect in the market. Soon enough, things will get more stable, and you can expect the prices to increase again. One thing to remember is that legal matters, especially the regulations imposed by states, have a strong influence on the price of bitcoin, as well as other cryptocurrencies. For example, when a news piece was released stating that South Korea was considering shutting down all its cryptocurrency exchanges, the price of bitcoin and all other cryptocurrencies experienced a significant decrease in price. This is nothing new; back in 2017, China also made a similar declaration, and the price of bitcoin and altcoins also experienced a drop in price. Once again, the lesson here is to consider how governments react to the use of cryptocurrencies, especially with regard to their legalities.

CHAPTER 2:
GETTING STARTED WITH BITCOIN

Now that you have a good idea of what bitcoin is, it is time for you to have an overview of how to get started with bitcoin so that you will know just what to expect. Well, the first step is to create a bitcoin wallet. There are basically just two types of bitcoin wallets: The hot and cold wallet. However, they are further divided into more specific types. Do not worry; they will be discussed in detail later on in this book. For now, you should learn what hot and cold wallets are.

Simply put, a hot wallet is a kind of bitcoin wallet that is stored completely online. As such, it is very easy and convenient to use. Hence, most cryptocurrency users use a hot wallet. All that you need to do is to sign up for an account for free from a wallet provider like *Coinbase*. The signing up process usually takes less than two minutes to complete. After which, you can now start using your bitcoin wallet. A cold wallet is the kind of bitcoin wallet where you store your private and public keys *offline*. Hence, to access your wallet and transfer funds, you will need to have your cold wallet in your possession. This is an added and highly effective security measure.

The next step is for you to own bitcoins. After all, the only way to invest and take advantage of bitcoin is by having bitcoins of your own. Although there are different ways to earn bitcoins, the quickest and fastest way to earn a good amount of bitcoins is by buying them. Bitcoin wallets like Coinbase will allow you to buy (and even sell) bitcoins directly from the wallet itself. This makes things very convenient for you. However, if the wallet that you use does not allow you to buy bitcoins, then you can simply sign up for a trading account with a cryptocurrency trading broker.

Again, creating an account is also fast and simple. However, it is important that you only work with a reliable and trusted broker. When you search online, you will surely find different brokers. As an investor, it is important that you only work with a reliable broker, so be sure to check the latest ratings and reviews of a broker prior to making any form of deposit.

Once you have bitcoins of your own, then you can keep them, and then sell them at a profit once they appreciate in value. However, the activity of investing in bitcoin is much more technical than just buying and selling bitcoin. After all, how do you know the right time to buy and sell bitcoin? Do not worry; all these will be discussed later in the book. For now, it is important for you to just have an idea of how you will get started.

As a bitcoin investor, you should know that research and analysis should be part of your day-to-day activity as an investor. Hence, before you even start to actually use and invest in bitcoin, you should already begin reading about the cryptocurrency market by now. Take note that bitcoin has many other competitors. Therefore, even though you may only intend to invest in bitcoin, it is still important that you keep an eye on its competitors, such as Ethereum, Litecoin, Ripple, Dash, and others. And, who knows, you might even be able to discover other profitable investment opportunities in the process.

CHAPTER 3:
UNDERSTANDING BLOCKCHAIN AND BITCOIN TRANSACTIONS

Before we discuss the specific steps on how you can profit by investing in bitcoin, you should first understand the technology behind bitcoin. Take note that the backbone technology of bitcoin is known as the *blockchain technology* or simply *blockchain*. What is blockchain? It is a public and decentralized distributed ledger which also acts as a repository of all transactions. It is made of records referred to as blocks. Before any block is added to the chain, it will undergo a strict process of verification and confirmation, which ensures that all the records that will be added to the chain are true and correct. Every new block is connected to the block that comes before it using what is known as a *hash pointer*. This way, all of the blocks in the blockchain network are interconnected with one another.

The blockchain is decentralized, which means that no organization exercises authority over it. It functions on its own free from any and all forms of influence and manipulation. This is why many people trust this system since there is no need for human intervention and control. The blockchain is also public, which means that all of the transactions are viewable to everyone on the network. This gives it added transparency and fairness and ensures that all transactions are legitimate and correct.

The blockchain technology is also an effective preventive measure against double spending and fraud, which are common problems in financial circles. When you use blockchain, there is absolutely no way to withdraw, modify, or cancel a transaction after it is confirmed. Not even Satoshi Nakamoto himself can stop or change it.

It also has a high level of security. Keep in mind that the blockchain network is spread over a wide connection of computers. For an attack against the blockchain system to be successful, the said attack has to possess at least 51% of the total hash rate of the entire bitcoin blockchain. Since the network is spread over a vast number of computers, achieving the said 51% can be considered as impossible. Take note that an attack with less than 51% hash rate is still possible, but you simply cannot expect for it to be successful. This is the idea behind the 51% attack concept.

It is noteworthy that bitcoin is not the only one that is gaining lots of attention and popularity. The blockchain technology has been making a name for itself apart from it being associated with bitcoin and other cryptocurrencies. This is because the blockchain has many other possible applications that are even well beyond the financial sector. Still, it can be said that blockchain is still a fairly new and young technology. Hence, there is still a room for improvement, and it is definitely something to keep an eye on.

How a Bitcoin Transaction Works

Every bitcoin transaction goes through a process. You should remember that there are 3 parts of a bitcoin transaction: Input, Output, and the Amount. Let us take a look at them one by one:

✓ Input

Let us say that person A wants to send 2 bitcoins to person B. Before person A can send B 2 bitcoins, it is only logical that person A must first have 2 bitcoins in his wallet. This is what is referred to as the *input*. Simply put, it refers to the bitcoins in the sender's wallet, the amount of which should be greater than or at least equal to the amount that he wants to send to another.

✓ Output

The output refers to the receiver. In our example, it is person B. More specifically, it refers to the *wallet address* of person B. Take note that in a bitcoin transaction, you do not send the bitcoin directly to the name of the receiver. In a blockchain, the transfer of bitcoins is made between wallet addresses. Hence, if you are the sender, then you should first ask for the bitcoin wallet address of the receiver. It is to this wallet address where you will send bitcoins.

✓ Amount

Obviously, this refers to the amount that is involved in a transaction. In this case, the amount is 2 bitcoins.

What about mining?

Mining refers to the process of verifying, confirming, and adding blocks or records to the blockchain. In a bitcoin transaction, once miners confirm a transaction, it can no longer be canceled, withdrawn, or modified. As you can see, mining is an important part of the blockchain ecosystem. Without mining, no new block or record can be added to the blockchain. Hence, in a bitcoin blockchain, you can rest assured that there is always a demand for miners.

CHAPTER 4:
WHERE TO KEEP YOUR BITCOIN

Now, let us move on to the more practical side: Do you keep or store your bitcoins? Remember that there are two kinds of bitcoin wallets: the hot and cold wallet. Now, these two main categories of bitcoin wallets are further classified into several specific types. You need to understand their differences so that you will know which wallet type will best suit your needs. Let us look at them one by one:

- *Online Wallet*

An online wallet is the most common type of bitcoin wallet. It is also known as a *web wallet*. This is the most commonly used type of bitcoin wallet as it is very easy and convenient to use. Good examples of an online wallet are Coinbase and GreenAddress. This is the type of wallet that you can easily access and manage simply by going online and logging in to your wallet through the site provided by your wallet provider. However, take note that this is a hot wallet, so you cannot expect for it to be a secured as a cold wallet. The good news is that many of the reputable hot wallets have already updated their security features. But, if security is your main concern, then a cold wallet is still the best choice.

- *Mobile Wallet*

A mobile wallet is another type of hot wallet. It is also an online wallet; but this time, you should download the wallet application on your mobile phone. Normally, you can download the application for free at the Apple and/or GooglePlay store. Many people use their phones to access the Internet, so having a mobile version of your wallet can be really handy at times. Do not worry; many web wallets like GreenAddress and Coinbase also have a mobile version of their bitcoin wallet.

• *Desktop Wallet*

A desktop wallet is a type of cold wallet. When you use a desktop wallet, you will store your public and private keys on a computer, which may also be a laptop computer. Before you use any computer as a desktop wallet, you should first reformat your computer or at least ensure that it is free from any malware and virus. Also, once you start using a computer as a cold wallet, you should no longer connect it to the Internet. This is what makes a cold wallet more secure than a hot wallet. Once something is exposed to the Internet, then it gets exposed to online hazards like hackers, attackers, and viruses. Since cold wallets are held offline, they are free from such risks. This is what makes a desktop wallet and other cold wallets very secured.

• *Hardware Wallet*

A hardware wallet functions just like a desktop wallet. But, instead of storing your public and private keys in a computer, you get to store them in a hardware. Although you can use an ordinary USB for this purpose, such is not advisable since an ordinary USB does not have enough protective features and can get easily get corrupted. Different kinds of hardware wallets are sold in the market specially made for this purpose, such as the Ledger Nano. However, they can get expensive. The good news is that to date, there has been no report or issue of any hardware wallet getting hacked or compromised. Hence, this is definitely one of the best bitcoin wallets that you can use in terms of having a very high level of security.

• *Paper Wallet*

A paper wallet is another famous type of cold wallet. When you use a paper wallet, you get to store your private and public keys on a paper. You can print them on paper. Ideally, you should keep several copies. Needless to say, you should store them in a safe place where they will not be stolen. Take note that although cold wallets offer high security, this is only as far as online hazards are concerned. They still cannot protect you from thieves or from losing or breaking your cold wallet.

Which wallet type should you use?

When choosing the right wallet for you, you need to strike a balance between security and convenience. For convenience, then any of the hot wallets would be a good choice. If you want to focus more on security, then you should use a cold wallet.

When choosing a wallet, you should think about how you intend to use your bitcoins. If you know that you will most likely transact with bitcoins on a regular basis, then you should use a hot wallet. However, if you just want to make a long-term investment where you just want to keep your bitcoins for a period of time, then using a cold wallet would be a better choice.

You are also free to use several wallet types at the same time. Hence, you can have a cold wallet and a hot wallet at the same time. You can use a hot wallet for short-term investments and for your day-to-day transactions, and then you can use a cold wallet at the same time for your long-term investment in bitcoin. There are also professional bitcoin investors who use multiple hot and cold wallets at the same time. You may find this necessary once you have a high number of bitcoins. After all, it is not advisable to keep all your bitcoins in a single wallet despite how secured you believe it to be. As they say, "Do not put all your eggs in one basket." The same is true when it comes to storing and keeping your bitcoins.

CHAPTER 5:
BUYING BITCOIN

How do you buy bitcoins? Buying bitcoins is easy. In fact, there are hot wallets like Coinbase and coins.ph will allow you to purchase bitcoins directly from the wallet itself. Now, if this is not possible, then you can sign up for a trading account with a cryptocurrency trading broker. There are brokers like eToro that will allow you to deposit fiat money and buy bitcoins on the trading platform itself. You may also want to use *localbitcoins*. It is like a marketplace where people buy and sell bitcoins. However, you need to be cautious when you use such kind of cryptocurrency marketplace as there are many scammers out there. Another popular option is to buy bitcoins using PayPal by through Virwox. However, take note that this is not a suggested approach as the cost can get very expensive. Hence, there are only two suggested ways to buy bitcoins: Through your bitcoin wallet and a trustworthy cryptocurrency trading broker.

Buy price vs. Sell price

Before you purchase bitcoins, you first need to understand that there is a difference between the buy price and the sell price. The buy price is always higher than the sell price. This difference in price is how a broker or seller makes a profit. This also means that right after you buy bitcoins, you cannot just sell them immediately after their price fluctuates a little higher as you will most probably end up with a loss since the sell price will be lower than the price at which you bought your bitcoins. Be sure to keep this in mind both when selling and buying bitcoins.

Check the market price

Before you buy and sell bitcoins, be sure to check its current price in the market. Do not forget that the price of Bitcoin fluctuates rapidly. This is to ensure that you are buying/selling your bitcoins at a fair price. A good way to do this is to visit the site of well-known cryptocurrency traders like Bitfinex, Binance, and Bittrex. You can also check well-established websites that share information about the cryptocurrency market, such as *coinmarketcap* and *coingecko*.

Timing

Do not just buy bitcoins right away. Before you make a purchase, you should first study the cryptocurrency market. Do not forget that bitcoin has a high volatility and that its price continuously changes. You definitely would not want to buy bitcoin when its price is falling down. Therefore, it is important that you study the market and use proper timing. Take note that the price of bitcoin rises and falls; hence, you may have to enter (buy) and leave (sell) the market every now and then, depending on the circumstances. By taking the effort to study the market, you will be able to save yourself some money and even lower your expenses and losses. Keep in mind that you do not just enter the market at any time you want. You need to be objective about it, and only buy bitcoins if you think that now is the moment to make a profitable investment. It is not uncommon for professional investors to wait for a day or even a week before they purchase bitcoins, even though they are eager to invest. Once again, proper timing is important when buying, as well as when selling bitcoins.

When selling bitcoins, you would want to sell them when their price is about to fall. However, this may also depend on your strategy. If you are making a long-term investment, then you should expect to face various price fluctuations in the market, and this includes facing some price decreases. Do not worry; in a long-term investment, the only important thing is to be at a profit once you close your position (when you sell your bitcoins). Hence, even if the price falls by 30% after two weeks, it would not matter if you can profit, say, by 100% the following week or so. Of course, you would not be investing blindly. To turn the odds in your favor and significantly increase your chances of making a profit, you will have to use effective strategies (as discussed later in this book).

CHAPTER 6:
USING BITCOIN

Using bitcoin is very easy and convenient. As we have already discussed, many merchants accept payments in bitcoin. Today, there are also many people around the world who use bitcoins for remittance or for sending funds to people located in another country. Since the use of bitcoin effectively cuts away the middleman like banks, it is a good way to minimize your cost. Now let us discuss what you need to do when you use bitcoins:

✓ **Sending bitcoins**

If you are the one who will send bitcoins, then all you need to do is ask for the bitcoin wallet address of the person to whom you intend to send bitcoins. A bitcoin wallet address looks like a long string of random letters and numbers. Be sure to copy and paste it correctly. Do not forget that once a transaction is confirmed, there is no way that you can cancel, amend, withdraw it. Therefore, be very careful when sending bitcoins. Be sure that you send it to the correct bitcoin wallet address. To send bitcoins, just access your wallet, key in the amount that you want to send, and then paste the wallet address of the recipient, and just click *send*. This entire process can be completed in less than a minute. As you can see, it is very simple. The recipient will soon be notified in his wallet that there is a pending receivable. Once the transaction has passed through several confirmations, then he will be able to finally receive the bitcoins that you send to his account. This normally takes just a few minutes from the time of sending the bitcoins.

✓ **Receiving bitcoins**

If you are the recipient, then you simply have to give your bitcoin wallet address to the sender. Again, to avoid committing mistakes, you should simply copy and paste your wallet address when sharing it with the sender.

✓ Storing bitcoins

We have already discussed the different ways to store your bitcoins. Make sure to keep your bitcoin wallet safe and secured. There are certain strongly suggested practices that you should observe, such as using a strong password and allowing the two-factor authentication. Keep in mind that your bitcoin wallet password is your main line of defense against a hacker or anyone who would want to access your account without your consent. To have a strong password, you should combine both upper and lower case letter. You should also use numbers and symbols in your password. Last but not least, avoid simply using the minimum required a number of characters. Instead, use a long password of at least 15 characters long. Needless to say, do not use a password that other people can easily guess. The two-factor authenticator is another line of defense that your account has. When you enable it, a code will be sent to your phone when anyone tries to access your account. Normally, you will have to enter this code after entering your password. The code changes within a few seconds, so it is very hard to predict correctly. You may have to download Google Authenticator app to be able to view the code. Do not worry; you can easily download this application for free from the GooglePlay or Apple store. If you are using a cold wallet, be sure to keep it in a safe place where it will not be broken or stolen.

CHAPTER 7:
INVESTING IN BITCOIN

Investing in bitcoin follows the usual trader's maxim: Buy low, sell high. However, this is easier said than done. To be able to invest successfully in bitcoin, you need to use effective strategies. Here are some notable strategies that you should learn and practice:

» *Fundamental Analysis*

Fundamental analysis is probably the most important strategy that you should learn. It is also referred as the lifeblood of investment. When you use fundamental analysis, you should focus on the *basics* or the fundamentals that affect bitcoin. Therefore, you should follow on the news and be up-to-date with the latest developments. The key to using this strategy is to gather as much good-quality information as you can. As they say, "Knowledge is power." It is a basic rule in investing that the more that you know and understand a certain asset, the more likely that you will be able to predict its price movement in the market. The same applies when you invest in bitcoin or any other cryptocurrency. When you use fundamental analysis, you should research and analyze the news, economy, competition among the different cryptocurrencies, market acceptance, and the past and current trend of bitcoin, among many others. Indeed, fundamental analysis is probably the strategy that takes a lot of effort, but it is well worth it. In fact, if you are serious about being a professional bitcoin investor, then it is a must that you should learn and use fundamental analysis. After all, this strategy can easily be incorporated even when you are using another strategy.

It is also strongly suggested that you should join online groups and forums about bitcoin and other cryptocurrencies. This is a good way to gather more information. From time to time, you will definitely learn some interesting ideas and strategies from these groups and forums. Since you are investing in bitcoin, be sure to join and participate in the *bitcointalk* forum. If you do not want to participate, then at least read the posts and learn something from them. It is also worth mentioning that many cryptocurrency developers are active in such kind of forums and groups, and this can allow you to gain valuable information against the competitors of bitcoin. Indeed, if you are serious about making continuous profit y investing in bitcoin or any other cryptocurrency, fundamental analysis is the strategy that you should always use.

» *Technical Analysis*

Technical analysis is a favorite among many bitcoin investors. This strategy is good if you are more of a visual person who loves to study and analyze graphs. When you use technical analysis, you will be looking at graphs and charts that reflect the price movements of bitcoin. The idea behind this strategy is that all of the elements or factors that affect the price of bitcoin can be summed up and have their final effect on the price. Therefore, this goes to show that simply by dealing with the price movements of bitcoin, you also get to deal with the many factors and elements that affect bitcoin. Of course, the advantage of using this approach is that it is much simpler than fundamental analysis where you need to research, read, and analyze so many pieces of information and even involves computations (numbers).

When you use technical analysis, the key is to be able to identify and take advantage of patterns. Yes, patterns do exist. However, they also come and go. Therefore, do not expect to see a pattern every time that you look at a graph or chart. A common mistake is to force to see a pattern even when there is actually no pattern to be seen. So, if you do not see a pattern, accept that it is not there and do not force an investment.

Technical analysis is a good strategy for short-term investments, while fundamental analysis is usually the choice when it comes to making long-term investments. Still, technical analysis is something that you can easily incorporate regardless of the strategy that you are using. After all, you simply have to view a chart or graph. Your trading broker will usually provide you with such tools (charts) that you need. If you do not have a trading broker, then there are many websites online that you can visit to see the price movements of bitcoin (as well as other cryptocurrencies).

Although you can use and depend completely on technical analysis, real experts suggest that you should still make use of fundamental analysis. The problem with technical analysis is that it does not give you the reasons behind the price movements; hence, you can barely come up with an accurate prediction. The best way to use technical analysis is still to combine it with fundamental analysis. If you use both strategies together properly, you can significantly increase your chances of making a profitable investment.

» *Averaging Down*

This is a good strategy to use if you want to be able to make a high amount of profit from an investment. This will allow you to purchase bitcoin at a "bargain" price. Here is an example of how to use this strategy: Let us say, for example, that the current price of bitcoin is $10,000. The first step is to make a buy order at its current price. Hence, you should buy bitcoin at the said price of $10,000. Now, if the price of bitcoin increases, then you make a profit. However, if the price of bitcoin drops, say, down to $9,500, then you should make another buy order at the said lower amount of $9,500. Now, if the price decreases again, then you should make another buy order. The key is simply to keep buying it while its price in decreasing. Hence, you get to buy bitcoin at a "bargain."

Okay, so this may seem like as if you are merely purchasing a losing asset, but this is actually not the case. Just imagine how much you will profit once the price of bitcoin recovers and goes back to its original price (the price when you first used this strategy), or even higher. All the buy orders that you have made will experience a nice profit. This is also an excellent strategy to use to take advantage of the volatility of the market.

Although this strategy is very practical and effective, do not forget that it is still considered an aggressive strategy. Hence, you should be careful when you use this approach. The proper way of using this strategy is to research the market first. Only use this strategy if you think that the price of bitcoin will most likely increase in the near future. If after doing your research and analysis, there are good reasons to believe that the price of bitcoin will most likely increase, then that is the only time that you should use this strategy.

» *Quick Sell*

This strategy is a good way to earn small yet consistent profits. The key to using this strategy is not to be greedy and close your position before your risk of exposure gets high. Here is an example of how you should use this strategy. Let us assume that the price of bitcoin is worth $10,000. You make a buy order at its current price of $10,000. Now, if the price increases, say, up to $10,200, then you should make a sell order right away and enjoy the small return of profits. Again, this is a good way to take advantage of a volatile market.

Take note, however, that the sell price is much lower than the buy price. Be sure to check the prevailing rate and only sell your bitcoin if you can make a profit out of it.

When you use this strategy, you should first study the market, especially the current trend of bitcoin. The best time to apply this strategy is while the price of bitcoin is increasing. Enter the market when it is hot and leave it even when it still appears to be profitable. The longer that you hold your position, the greater is your exposure to risk. Do not forget that when you use this strategy, you should prioritize controlling your risk. Hence, be contented with a small profit, and then start over.

» *Wait It Out*

There are times when it can be difficult to invest in bitcoin. For example, as of the start of 2018, the price of bitcoin has been unstable. This does not mean that it is no longer a good investment. Rather, this only shows that it may not be a good time to invest in bitcoin at the moment. Again, this is part of the usual fluctuations that you can expect when you deal with any kind of cryptocurrency/ however, you can rest assured that this will soon change (which is part of the nature of the cryptocurrency market). So, do not be like the other investors who keep on investing even when the market is down. To minimize your risk and losses, you should only invest in bitcoin when it is profitable in the market. But, when you see that its price has constantly been falling for days and weeks, the best action would be to just be patient and keep watch. Soon, bitcoin will again be able to recover, and that is the time for you to invest as its price continues to increase.

Remember that no matter how eager you are to invest in bitcoin, you must be patient to wait for the right opportunity. The important thing is that you are ready to invest once that opportunity arises. Therefore, it is your job to continue to follow and study the market. Wait out the bad times and join the hot streaks. Pay close attention to the market.

» *Go with the Flow*

Bitcoin is not really that hard to predict. For example, when it was announced in the news that China would close down all its local cryptocurrency exchanges, bitcoin and altcoins experienced a drop in price. However, when the news featured that Russia started to legalize bitcoins, the price of bitcoin surged upwards. The same is true when bitcoin was featured on CNN showing just how profitable an investment it is. Again, when Singapore declared that it would not issue any restriction yet on bitcoin, the price of bitcoin also increased. As you can see, sometimes you just have to go with the flow, and you can easily make a profit. Bitcoin is not always hard to predict. In fact, most of the time, it is very easy to predict the direction that its price movement will take in the market.

When you go with the flow, it is still advised that you do your fundamental analysis to be sure that you are not being misdirected. Sometimes what you read online or see in the news can be deceiving, especially when there is a pump and dump scheme. What is a pump and dump scheme? This fraudulent scheme is nothing new. In fact, it has been used in the stock market for years and is now being used in the cryptocurrency market. In a pump and dump scheme, a group of people will promote a certain cryptocurrency using some form of promotional hype. Their objective is to draw as much as positive attention and interest as possible to drive the price of the promoted cryptocurrency higher. However, once its price increases as other investors continue to make investments thinking that it is a profitable cryptocurrency, the people behind the scheme will then sell the cryptocurrency being promoted at a nice profit. The final result is that those behind the scheme can make a good profit while the investors (victims of the scheme) will be holding a losing asset. Hence, for you not to fall victim to this scheme, be sure to do your own analysis of the market and do not just follow the flow without doing any research.

CHAPTER 8:
BITCOIN FOR BUSINESS

Businesses around the world also use Bitcoin. In fact, by using bitcoin in business, you can effectively cut down your cost as you would no longer need a middleman like banks and other financial sectors for sending and receiving money (cryptocurrency) to another. You have full control of everything. The process, as we have already discussed, is also very quick and simple. Indeed, many businesses use and accept bitcoins. Let us look at some of these known businesses that use bitcoin:

• *Microsoft*

Microsoft needs no introduction. This computer giant is known worldwide, and now it is also known for accepting payments in bitcoin when you buy from Windows or Xbox store.

• *Virgin Galactic*

This company engaged in space travel also accepts bitcoin. So, if you have lots of bitcoins in your possession, you can now buy your trip to space. The founder of Virgin Galactic openly admitted that he supports bitcoin cryptocurrency.

• *Wikipedia*

As you know, Wikipedia is a huge website where you can get tons of valuable information for free. Anyone who uses the Internet is familiar with Wikipedia. Well, although you can use Wikipedia for free, it is also known for accepting donations in bitcoin.

• *Tesla*

If you are interested in science and technology, perhaps you would also find it interesting to know that the company, Tesla, also uses and accepts payment in bitcoin. In fact, some of its inventions were funded using bitcoins.

• *Peach Airlines*

The Japanese airline known as Peach Airline also accepts payment in bitcoin. So, if you want to travel to another country and would love to pay for your airfare using bitcoins, you might want to buy your ticket from Peach Airlines

• *Steam*

Steam is a popular gaming platform with millions of registered and active users. You can now buy games and upgrades using bitcoins.

• *Overstock*

This company allows you to purchase big-ticket items. You can now buy products from Overstock using bitcoins. In fact, they have even partnered with a famous bitcoin wallet known as *Coinbase*.

Many other companies and businesses use and accept payments in bitcoin. Now, if you own a business, you can also take advantage of bitcoins by paying your employees in bitcoins. Just be sure to check if this is allowed in the laws of your country. Also, if your business normally involves sending and receiving funds, then you should really consider using bitcoins as it can effectively lower your expenses and will allow you to have complete control of the process. It is also good to use bitcoins if you are to send "money" to someone who is located in another country. The bitcoin system is open 24 hours a day every day; hence, you can easily send and receive bitcoins with just a few clicks of a mouse. If you are the recipient, then simply give your bitcoin wallet address to the sender, and just wait for him to send your bitcoins into your wallet.

CHAPTER 9:
BITCOIN MINING

Mining bitcoins is another investment that you might want to consider. As we have already discussed, there is always a demand for miners in the bitcoin blockchain; otherwise, there is no way for any record or transaction to be added to the chain and be completed. Now, there are different ways to mine bitcoins. Let us go over them one by one:

- *Computer mining*

This is the most basic way to mine for bitcoins. This is where you use your own computer for mining. You can do this by downloading GUIMiner and joining a mining pool. The suggested pool is the Slush's pool. However, this is only a good method to give you an experience of mining, but it is not a recommended method if you want to earn a decent amount of bitcoins. The reason is that a computer alone does not have sufficient hash power to mine a decent amount of bitcoins. You will most probably end up with more expenses on electricity than the actual amount of bitcoin that you could mine. Also, when you mine using your own computer, you will have to worry about overheating. Take note of this because this can break your computer's CPU. So, when it comes to earning a decent amount of bitcoins, this is not a recommended method. But, if you just want to experience how it feels like to mine bitcoins and earn a little, then this is a good start.

- *Hardware mining*

Since a computer alone is not enough to mine a decent amount of bitcoins due to its low mining power, you will have to use a mining hardware to increase your hash or mining power. There are websites online like Amazon and eBay where you can buy a mining hardware. It is noteworthy that even if you mine using a hardware, you still have to use your computer. Hence, you should still be careful about any overheating issues. You should follow a schedule that will allow your computer and mining hardware to cool down from time to time. In choosing a hardware, you should look at the mining power and also the electric consumption. It is not uncommon to find a strong mining hardware but then also consumes high electricity. You need to consider this to ensure that you will end up with a decent positive profit.

- *Could mining*

This seems to be the most famous method of mining bitcoins nowadays. With cloud mining, you no longer have to worry about any overheating issue. You do not even have to purchase any mining hardware. In fact, you do not even have to mine anything at all. Hence, you do not even have to use your computer. Instead, all that you need to do is to wait for the cloud mining company to send you bitcoins. You will usually receive your bitcoins every week or as soon as you meet the minimum threshold. Okay, this may sound too good to be true, so what is the catch? Of course, there is also a catch. After all, you cannot expect for any business to send you bitcoins every week just out of kindness. The catch is that you will first have to invest. This means that you must first pay a cloud mining company. Now, you have to be careful about this because there are many scammers online who simply want to rip you off of your money. Therefore, before you invest in any cloud mining company, you need to do your research, check the latest reviews given to the mining company, and learn as much as you can about the said company.

A usual offer may look something like this: Invest (or pay) 1 bitcoin and earn up to 0.035 bitcoins every week. Okay, so far this seems very ideal. You just have to make some simple computation, and you would already know when you can recover your investment, and then you can earn positive profits after that. However, this is not always the case. The problem is that the offer only shows the *expected* return and not the actual return of profits. This means that using the given example, you may receive less than 0.035 every week. Before you make any form of deposit or investment, you need to be sure that the terms and agreements of the contract are clear to you. In case of doubts, do not hesitate the customer support team, and they would be happy to assist you. Also, pay attention to the expiration date. There are cloud mining companies that only render the contract valid for a year — and so this means that you should be able to recover your investment and then earn profits within the same time period. Other cloud mining companies honor a lifetime validity of contract. Again, the best way to be sure about this is to read the contract and talk with the customer support team of the cloud mining company for clarifications.

CHAPTER 10:
SECURITY OF BITCOIN

So, is it safe and secure to use bitcoin? The answer is *yes*. Otherwise, companies would no longer be using it in business. Although there were reports in the past that certain bitcoin wallets had been hacked, it is worth noting that the security of both hot and cold wallets has already improved significantly. In fact, many professional investors these days only use a hot wallet or the trading account provided by their cryptocurrency trading broker. The point here is that in terms of security, you can rest assured that bitcoin has a high level of security. Also, do not forget the 51% attack concept. Today, bitcoin is well distributed over a very vast network of computers, so just imagine how much hash rate power an attacker needs to have to penetrate the bitcoin blockchain successfully.

As an investor, you no longer need to worry whether or not bitcoin is secure because it is. Your main concern is how to ensure the security of your bitcoin wallet. As we have already discussed, you may want to use a cold wallet for this purpose. If you are using a hot wallet, be sure to enhance the security of your wallet by using a strong password and also activate the two-factor authentication or any other security features that your wallet provider may offer.

Bitcoin is also a continuously evolving technology, so you can expect for its security features to get even stronger and more secure over time. The good news is that as far as security is concerned, it can now be said that bitcoin is very secure. Hence, so many individuals and known businesses are using it, and many are still eager to learn about it so that they can also take advantage of the benefits of using bitcoin. In fact, there are those who believe that bitcoin is even more secure than traditional banks. As bitcoin continues to grow and dominate the cryptocurrency market, you can expect for more developments and improvements to happen over time.

CONCLUSION

Thanks for making it through to the end of this book. We hope it was informative and able to provide you with all of the tools you need to achieve your goals whatever they may be.

The next step is to apply everything that you have learned and start earning serious profits. Unfortunately, many people still think that bitcoin is a bubble that is about to burst. Well, it is up to you whether or not you want to believe this heresy. However, as far as the truth is concerned, those who believe that bitcoin is just a bubble failed to make any profit from it, while those who have taken the risk and believe in bitcoin as a profitable investment can earn a high amount of profits, even their way to complete financial freedom.

Finally, if you found this book useful in anyway, a review on Amazon is always appreciated!

CRYPTOCURRENCY INVESTING

The Ultimate Guide About Top Cryptocurrencies for Investing and Perfect Strategies to Make Money

By Sam Sutton

~~~

© Copyright 2018 By Sam Sutton
All Rights Reserved

The transmission, duplication or reproduction of any of the following work including specific information will be considered an illegal act irrespective of if it is done electronically or in print. This extends to creating a secondary or tertiary copy of the work or a recorded copy and is only allowed with express written consent from the Publisher. All additional right reserved.

The information in the following pages is broadly considered to be a truthful and accurate account of facts and as such any inattention, use or misuse of the information in question by the reader will render any resulting actions solely under their purview. There are no scenarios in which the publisher or the original author of this work can be in any fashion deemed liable for any hardship or damages that may befall them after undertaking information described herein. This book should not be taken as financial or investment advice, and the author does not take any responsibility for inaccuracies, omissions, or errors which may be found therein.

Additionally, the information in the following pages is intended only for informational purposes and should thus be thought of as universal. As befitting its nature, it is presented without assurance regarding its prolonged validity or interim quality. Trademarks that are mentioned are done without written consent and can in no way be considered an endorsement from the trademark holder.

The contents of this book are intended to convey general information only. You should not treat any information herein as a call to make any particular decision regarding cryptocurrency usage, legal matters, investments, taxes, cryptocurrency mining, exchange usage, wallet usage, etc. It is strongly suggested that you seek advice from your own financial, investment, tax, or legal adviser. This book should not be taken as financial or investment advice, and the author does not take any responsibility for inaccuracies, omissions, or errors. The author of this work is not responsible for any loss, damage, or inconvenience caused as a result of reliance on information as published on, or linked to, this book.

The author of this book has taken careful measures to share vital information about the subject. May its readers acquire the right knowledge, wisdom, inspiration, and succeed.

TABLE OF CONTENTS

Introduction 53

Chapter 1: Myths About Cryptocurrency Market and
Main Rules of the Market 55

Chapter 2: Basic Principles of Cryptocurrency 61

Chapter 3: Mining Cryptocurrency and
How the Mining Process Works 67

Chapter 4: Blockchain Technology 71

Chapter 5: Wallets and How to Securely Store Bitcoin 73

Chapter 6: Top 10 Cryptocurrencies and
Where to Track Them 79

Chapter 7: Most Popular Cryptocurrency Exchanges 83

Chapter 8: Investment strategies 87

Conclusion 91

INTRODUCTION

Congratulations on downloading this book and thank you for doing so.

The following chapters will teach you everything that you need to know about investing in cryptocurrencies. They will provide you with the right knowledge that will allow you to join the cryptocurrency race, turn the odds in your favor, and dominate the cryptocurrency market. This is your chance to rake in serious and continuous profits.

Chapter 1 talks about the myths that surround the cryptocurrency market and reveals the main rules orfacts behind them.

Chapter 2 discusses the basic rules that you need to know when you invest in cryptocurrency.

Chapter 3 talks about mining cryptocurrency and how the mining process works.

Chapter 4 explains the blockchain technology, which is the backbone technology of bitcoin and other cryptocurrencies.

Chapter 5 explains the different kinds of cryptocurrency wallets, as well as how to securely store your bitcoin or any other cryptocurrency.

Chapter 6 talks about the top 10 cryptocurrencies in the market and where you can track them.

Chapter 7 discusses the most popular cryptocurrency exchanges that you can use to buy, sell, or trade cryptocurrencies.

Chapter 8 reveals powerful and effective investment strategies that you can use to turn the odds in your favour and significantly increase your chances of making high and continuous profits.

May this book be your guiding light to success and financial freedom.

There are plenty of books on this subject on the market, thanks again for choosing this one! Every effort was made to ensure it is full of as much useful information as possible. Please enjoy!

CHAPTER 1:
MYTHS ABOUT CRYPTOCURRENCY MARKET AND MAIN RULES OF THE MARKET

There are myths that surround the cryptocurrency market. As an investor, it is important for you to know the truth behind the myths in order for you to have the right view and understanding of the cryptocurrency market. Let us uncover the facts behind these popular myths one by one:

- *Myth #1: Cryptocurrencies are a big bubble that is about to burst.*

For years, many people have viewed bitcoin and other cryptocurrencies as a mere bubble that is about to burst. Because of this fear, which arises from an erroneous perception, they fail to take advantage of the cryptocurrency market, while those who have the will to take risks and believe in cryptocurrencies have been able to earn a high amount of profit. In fact, some of them have even made their way to complete financial freedom simply by investing in cryptocurrencies like bitcoin, Ethereum, and others. Still, even today, there are those who say that cryptocurrencies are just a bubble. Well, it is up to you if you are going to believe those who claim that it is a bubble. However, the fact remains that while other people think that cryptocurrencies are a mere bubble, there are those who take the risks and believe in the power and value that cryptocurrencies offer, and they are able to rake in serious profits. Whether a bubble or not, it is true that investing in cryptocurrencies can be a very lucrative investment.

The main rule of the market dictates that a cryptocurrency will only "burst" if it has no value or loses its value. But there is no "bubble" to talk about it. This is because bitcoin offers real value to the market. It is widely recognized as a cryptocurrency that can be used for trading.

- ***Myth #2: Unlike the U.S. dollar, cryptocurrencies have no real value.***

Years ago, the value of the U.S. dollar was pegged to the value or price of gold. However, the dollar was soon weaned off of gold. The result was that the dollar did not have anything to back itself except the faith of the people in its value. The same applies when you use cryptocurrencies. It is the faith of the people that a certain cryptocurrency has a value that allows it to continue to have value and importance in the market. Also, it is noteworthy that many cryptocurrencies these days do not just function as mere substitute for money. In fact, they offer something that makes them even more valuable. For example, the altcoin Ethereum promotes the use of smart contracts and distributed applications on its blockchain. Another example is Ripple, which actually helps banks to have quicker transactions at a lower cost. So, as far as value is concerned, it can easily be said that cryptocurrencies, especially those that are in the mainstream, are highly valuable.

- ***Myth #3: Cryptocurrencies are for criminals.***

Due to the anonymity enjoyed by cryptocurrency users, there are people who think that cryptocurrencies are primarily created and used for illegal activities like money laundering. However, this is not true. Although cryptocurrency users enjoy a high level of anonymity, they still do not have complete anonymity. This is why those who abused the use of cryptocurrencies to commit illegal acts have already been arrested. Also, if you look at the facts, those who buy guns and other weapon often use fiat money (the official currency of a state) and not cryptocurrencies. Fiat money has been used in illegal activities for many years. This happens even today, especially in the black market.

- ***Myth #4: Investing in cryptocurrencies will only make you lose your investment in the long run.***

Just like any other investment, there are risks involved when you invest in any cryptocurrency. Hence, it is true that you might lose your investment, just as you can also easily lose your investment when you put your money in the stock market, especially if you do not know the ins and outs of the market. In any kind of investment, there are those who make a nice profit and there are also those who lose a part of or even their whole investment. Nonetheless, when you invest in cryptocurrencies, you may or may not lose your investment. In fact, there are so many cryptocurrency investors who have earned a very high amount of profit. Remember the classic example: Had you invested even just $400 in bitcoins back in 2009 or 2010, then you would have earned millions in profit by now. There are many real-life success stories of people who have earned millions in profit. In fact, there are many cryptocurrency investors who have earned their way to financial freedom.

- ***Myth #5: Investing in cryptocurrencies is a fast and easy way to make money.***

Now, there are also those who think that investing in cryptocurrency is a quick and easy way that leads to financial freedom. However, the truth is that even though there are people who have earned millions of dollars and attained financial freedom by simply investing in cryptocurrencies, they are not an everyday occurrence. Many professional and successful traders spend hours on a daily basis just studying the highly volatile cryptocurrency market, and they are very careful whenever they enter or leave a position. Most successful cryptocurrency traders are highly meticulous to details and are very careful with their investment decisions. If you are serious about having continuous success and profit in the cryptocurrency market, then it is a basic rule that you should do hours of research and analysis. Keep in mind that you are dealing with a quickly evolving and highly competitive market

• Myth #6: *The blockchain can easily be hacked.*

Here is the truth: Nobody has ever successfully hacked the blockchain. You may read reports of various cryptocurrency wallets being hacked, but those do not refer to the blockchain network itself. The blockchain is a highly secure system and network that is spread over a vast number of computers. Of course, an attack against the blockchain is possible; however, for an attack against the blockchain to be successful, then the attack must possess at least 51% of the hash power of the entire blockchain network. Needless to say, since blockchain is spread over a vast network of computers, obtaining the said 51% is virtually impossible.

Another bit of good news is that cryptocurrency wallets have already upgraded their security features. In fact, these days, you could barely hear any news of any cryptocurrency being hacked, especially if the person observes certain protective measures, such as using a strong password and enabling two-factor authentication, among others. If you still worry about the security of your cryptocurrency wallet, then you can always use a cold wallet to completely protect it from hackers, malware, and viruses.

• Myth #7: *Governments will prohibit the use of cryptocurrencies.*

The general rule is that the use of cryptocurrencies is legal. If you look at the facts, it is easy to see that almost all governments allow the use of cryptocurrencies in their respective jurisdictions. Over time, more and more states become open to the idea of finally using and embracing cryptocurrencies. A good example of this is Russia, which used to outlaw the use of cryptocurrencies in its territory. In 2017, Russia legalized the use of bitcoins and other cryptocurrencies. Although China closed down all of its local cryptocurrency exchanges, it was for the purpose of preparing some regulations on the use of cryptocurrencies, not for the purpose of permanently isolating itself from the cryptocurrency market. Singapore declared that it would not yet impose any regulation on the use of cryptocurrencies. In many countries, like in the U.S., Canada, Europe, India, Philippines, and many others, the use of bitcoins and other cryptocurrencies is legal. In fact, cryptocurrencies are only prohibited in a very few countries, such as in Ecuador, Bolivia, and Kyrgyzstan, and few others.

Some say that the people behind these cryptocurrencies will soon be arrested. It should be noted that cryptocurrencies like bitcoin are decentralized. This means that there is no person, organization, or authority that exercises control over it. The system works on its own. Hence, there is no one that can be arrested or be put on trial.

- *Myth #8: It is hard to understand the cryptocurrency market.*

Of course, if you read the white paper of a cryptocurrency, you will most likely find it hard to understand because of the technical terms that are used. But cryptocurrencies are easy to understand as long as you are willing to learn and engage in research. For example, by the time that you finish reading this book alone, you will already be equipped with the right knowledge of what cryptocurrencies are about, as well as how you can make an investment and earn a nice profit. In fact, investing in stocks is much more technical than understanding and investing in cryptocurrencies. If you can devote several hours and if you are truly willing to learn, then you can rest assured that you will be able to understand the ins and outs of cryptocurrencies in no time.

So, there you have it. These are the popular myths that surround the cryptocurrency market. Now that you know the truth behind the myths, it is time for you to know the basic principles that govern these cryptocurrencies, so that you will have a much better understanding of what cryptocurrencies really are.

CHAPTER 2:
BASIC PRINCIPLES OF CRYPTOCURRENCY

What is a *Cryptocurrency*?

A *cryptocurrency* is a type of digital asset. It has no physical existence. Instead, it is stored and held electronically (online). It is "crypto" because it is secured using *cryptography*, which refers to the practice of converting information into codes in order to ensure secure communication. Cryptography was used during the Second World War when it was extremely important for the army to ensure that their communications and correspondences were protected against enemy spies. It is a "currency" in the sense that it functions as a substitute for money. Hence, you can use it to buy certain products and services from merchants who accept cryptocurrencies, such as Microsoft, Steam, Peach Airlines, Virgin Galactic, Fiverr, and Overstock, among many others. To date, there are over a thousand different cryptocurrencies in the market, and the number keeps on increasing.

Cryptocurrency vs. Fiat money

Although a cryptocurrency like bitcoin may be used as a medium of exchange, it is still not considered as *fiat money*. What is fiat money? Fiat money refers to the official currency of a state, which is regulated by its government. An excellent example of fiat money is the U.S. dollar. This is because a cryptocurrency is decentralized, which means that there is no person or group that exercises authority over it. This makes it free from all forms of manipulation and undue advantage. Since cryptocurrency is not considered fiat money, it is also not considered *legal tender*. Legal tender refers to that which a "debtor may compel a creditor to accept payment." Of course, the exception to this is if payment in cryptocurrency is agreed upon by the parties in their contract.

It is noteworthy that although a cryptocurrency is neither fiat money nor legal tender, it is still widely accepted by numerous businesses and individuals around the world. In fact, over time, the number of cryptocurrency users has been constantly increasing. Indeed, so many people these days are very eager to learn and understand how to use (and invest) in cryptocurrency.

Bitcoin vs. Altcoins

Bitcoin is the number one cryptocurrency in the world. Back in 2008, a paper was published on a cryptography mailing list. The paper was entitled *Bitcoin: A Peer-to-Peer Electronic Cash System* under the name Satoshi Nakamoto. The following year, bitcoin was finally launched in the market. Back then, bitcoin did not have any substantial value. In fact, just like all other cryptocurrencies (altcoins), it was the cryptocurrency community members themselves who decided the value of bitcoin. There was even a transaction where two pizzas delivered by Papa John's were bought for 10,000 bitcoins. You can still see how this transaction took place on the *bitcointalk* forum, and you will also see other comments that obviously reflect that the people did not take bitcoin seriously at that time. Today, bitcoin is the most successful and highly-priced cryptocurrency in the world. As of January 18, 2018, the price of 1 bitcoin is around $11,600 USD.

To date, there are more than 1,000 different cryptocurrencies in the market. Still, bitcoin is recognized as the number one and most successful cryptocurrency in the world. In fact, it has so strongly established itself that it is now considered as the leading standard of all cryptocurrencies to the point that all other cryptocurrencies are merely called as *altcoins*, which is short for *alternative coins*.

However, it is noteworthy that investing in altcoins can also be a highly lucrative investment. For example, in 2017, the altcoin known as OmisgeGO increased by more than 1,200% in price in just several weeks. Also in 2017, the altcoin, Ethereum, which is the second most successful cryptocurrency in the market and is currently the next in rank to bitcoin, increased by over 13,000%.

Anonymity

Cryptocurrency users enjoy a high level of anonymity. In a transaction, the name and other personal details of the parties involved remain private. Instead of revealing personal details, only the cryptocurrency wallet address, amount involved, and the time stamp are usually the things that are shown to the public. Hence, if privacy is a concern, you will definitely find using cryptocurrencies very helpful.In fact, some cryptocurrencies like Zcash and Dash will allow you to almost completely hide or make private your transaction.

How a cryptocurrency transaction works

A cryptocurrency transaction may not always work the same way, depending on how its blockchain system is structured. However, the usual cryptocurrency transaction, such as when you use bitcoins, has three main parts:

✓ Input

Before anyone can send any cryptocurrency to another, it is only logical that he must first have enough cryptocurrency to send in his cryptocurrency wallet. This means that he must first receive cryptocurrency from another. This is what is referred to as an *input*. Once you have an input, then you can start sending or using cryptocurrency.

✓ Output

The output refers to the recipient's cryptocurrency wallet address. Take note that a single cryptocurrency wallet can generate multiple different addresses. The *output* refers to the wallet address of the recipient that will receive the cryptocurrency that you will send.

✓ Amount

The *amount*, of course, refers to the amount involved in a transaction; therefore, if you are going to send 1 bitcoin, then the *amount* involved in the transaction is 1 bitcoin.

Additional notes

When you are the one who is sending cryptocurrency to another, be sure that you get the right cryptocurrency wallet address. Every cryptocurrency wallet address is unique from the others. It looks like a string of randomly-generated letters and numbers. Once a transaction is confirmed, there is no way that you can cancel or change it, so make sure that you send the cryptocurrency to the correct wallet address. Sending cryptocurrency is fast and easy, especially if you are using a hot wallet. If you are using a cold wallet, then this might take a longer time. The different types of cryptocurrency wallets will be discussed later in the book.If you are the recipient (receiver), then all that you need to do is to give your cryptocurrency wallet address to the sender and wait for him to send you cryptocurrency.

Why Invest in Cryptocurrency?

It is true that although a cryptocurrency functions as a substitute for money, the majority of cryptocurrency holders do not use it as a medium of exchange. Instead, they buy and sell cryptocurrency as a form of investment. Is it lucrative enough? Well, just remember the classic example: Had you invested even just $400 in bitcoin back in 2009 or early 2010, then you would have earned multimillion dollars in profit by now. Needless to say, bitcoin is not the only cryptocurrency in the market that is worth investing in. There are also many altcoins in the market whose price surge as high as 2,000% (and even way higher) in just a short span of time. So, is it profitable to invest in cryptocurrency? The answer is a resounding *yes*. However, just like any other investment, there are also risks involved when you invest in cryptocurrency, and this includes the risk of losing your whole investment. This is the reason why professional and successful cryptocurrency investors use strategies. When you use effective and powerful strategies, you can significantly increase your chances of making the right investment decision. Do not worry; these strategies are also revealed in this book. So, just keep on reading and learning, and you will soon gain a strong foundation to be able to dominate the cryptocurrency market and use it to your advantage. One thing is certain: If you are serious about making continuous profit by investing in a cryptocurrency or different types of cryptocurrencies, then you should be willing to spend hours in research. Just like anything that is worth pursuing, success in the cryptocurrency market requires time, efforts, practice, and hard work.

High volatility

The cryptocurrency market is known for having high volatility. What is *high volatility*? It means that the price of a cryptocurrency usually rises and falls rapidly and significantly. This allows its price to fluctuate and increase by more than 50% (or higher) in 24 hours. Of course, the opposite is also true, which means that its price can drop quickly. This is why you need to study and analyze the market, so that you will be more able to predict the price direction that a particular cryptocurrency will take. Indeed, the cryptocurrency market has a very high volatility. In fact, this is the reason why some investors are afraid to invest in ay cryptocurrency since a market with a high volatility also involves a high risk. However, if you come to think about it, it is not really something that you should be discouraged of. You have to realize that it is exactly the high volatile nature of the cryptocurrency market that makes it a very lucrative investment. It is exactly why you could profit by more than 20,000% in a short span of time. Although there are risks involved, as can be expected of any worthy investment, there are strategies that you can use to turn the odds in your favor and significantly increase your chances of making a highly profitable investment.

CHAPTER 3:
MINING CRYPTOCURRENCY AND HOW THE MINING PROCESS WORKS

Let us discuss another interesting topic in the world of cryptocurrency known as *mining*. Mining is another investment option that you have when you deal with cryptocurrencies. So, what is *mining*? Mining refers to the process of verifying and adding transactions or blocks on the blockchain. The blockchain is the central technology of bitcoin and other cryptocurrencies. It is composed of a record of transactions known as *blocks*. There is a constant demand for miners because without the miners, no new record or block can be added to the blockchain. This means that no transaction can be completed. Hence, mining is a very important activity.

How Does It Work?

Before any new record is added to the blockchain, it must first undergo a process of confirmation and verification. This is what mining is all about. The first thing that a miner does is to verify whether or not a certain transaction is valid or not. Next, a miner will bundle the recent transactions into a block. After that, the miner selects the header of the latest block and connects it to the new block as a hash. The next step is the most difficult part, and that is to solve the Proof of Work (PoW). This is where a miner solves a difficult mathematical puzzle. Once the miner is able to find a solution to the puzzle, only then will the block be added to the blockchain. Hence, this is the time when a transaction will be fully completed. Miners are compensated usually in the form of a transaction fee every time they are able to mine a block. This is the usual way that mining works. Of course, depending on how the system of a certain cryptocurrency is structured, the mining procedure may have some differences.

How to Mine Cryptocurrency

There are several ways to mine cryptocurrency. Let us discuss them one by one:

✓ Computer Mining

You can use your computer to mine cryptocurrency. This is also known as CPU mining, since you will be mining using the power of your computer's CPU. This is a good way to experience what it feels like to actually mine cryptocurrency. You simply have to download the software, and then you can use your computer to start mining. There are free mining software options that you can download online. A popular mining software that you can use is the GUIMiner. It should be noted that you cannot expect to earn a decent amount of cryptocurrency if you only mine using your computer alone. The reason is that a computer does not have sufficient mining power to mine blocks quickly. You will most probably end up with more electricity expenses than the total amount of cryptocurrency that you can mine. Hence, only consider computer mining as way to partake of the actual mining experience, but do not expect to earn any profit from it. Also, when you use computer mining, you should be cautious of overheating problems. You should pay attention to this since too much overheating may break your computer. Be sure to give enough time for your computer to cool down.

✓ Hardware Mining

Since a computer alone does not generate enough mining power to earn you a decent amount of cryptocurrency, the better approach is to do hardware mining. Hardware mining makes use of hardware in order to increase your mining hash power. There are various mining hardware options that you can find online. You might want to check Amazon and eBay. Take note that even if you use hardware, you will still have to use your computer. Hence, you should still be careful with overheating issues. Be sure to give your computer and your hardware enough time to cool down. A major drawback of using this mining approach is that good-quality mining hardware can be expensive, and it will take time before you can fully recover your expenses and break even. In choosing your mining hardware, you should pay attention to the mining power and the electricity consumption. Figure out the necessary computation to see how much you will most likely earn. It is not uncommon to find a bit of strong mining hardware that also spends much electric power. And it is worth repeating that you should pay attention to any overheating issues.

✓ **Cloud Mining**

Cloud mining is probably the most popular and recommended method of mining cryptocurrency these days. When you use cloud mining, you will no longer have to worry about purchasing any hardware or any overheating issue. You do not even have to use your computer. In fact, you do not even have to mine cryptocurrency. All that you need to do is to relax and wait for your mining company to send to you your cryptocurrency, which is usually on a weekly basis or as soon as you reach the minimum threshold amount. Okay, this seems too good to be true. So, what is the catch? The catch is that before a cloud mining company begins to mine for you, you must first make an investment (pay the cloud mining company). A typical offer may look like this: Invest 0.5 bitcoins and receive 0.008 bitcoins every week. At first glance, this seems like a really good deal. You just need to do a simple computation, and you will be able to tell when you will recover your investment, and then the profits that you can earn. However, the problem here is that the offer is usually just the *expected* return and does not refer to the actual return that you will receive. Therefore, there is the possibility that you might receive less than the agreed amount. In our given example, it could be less than 0.008 bitcoins every week. Not to mention, there have been reports where investors did not receive any payment or profit from their cloud mining company. Therefore, be careful since there are many scammers out there. It is important that you only work with a trustworthy and reliable mining company. Before you invest or make any form of deposit, be sure to check the latest ratings and reviews given to the cloud mining company.

It is also not uncommon for cloud mining companies to fix an expiration date to the contract. Hence, you should be able to get back your investment and also make a good amount of profit before the contracts expires. Once the contract expires, then the cloud mining company will no longer mine for you. In order to renew the contract, you will have to pay the mining company again. It is noteworthy that some cloud mining companies may allow you to have a lifetime contract with them. Just be sure to check the terms and conditions of the contract. As can be expected, those that offer a lifetime contract will most likely be the ones that will offer a low return. Regardless of the duration of the mining contract, make sure to read and understand all of the provisions in the contract. This is also a good time for you to hire a good lawyer to make sure that the contract is fair and reasonable before you make any investment, especially if you intend to make a big investment.

Although mining cryptocurrency can still be a highly profitable activity, many experts advise that if you want a better way to earn cryptocurrency and without any limitation to the profit that you can earn, then you should learn investing directly on cryptocurrencies instead of mining them. There are different investing strategies that you can use to increase your chances of making a high amount of profit, as revealed in this book.

CHAPTER 4:
BLOCKCHAIN TECHNOLOGY

Blockchain technology, or simply known as *blockchain*, is the backbone technology of bitcoin and other cryptocurrencies. The first decentralized and public blockchain was developed by Satoshi Nakamoto, the man behind the number one cryptocurrency of all, bitcoin. Bitcoin, as well as other cryptocurrencies, uses the blockchain technology. So, what exactly is this blockchain technology? Blockchain is a public, decentralized, and distributed ledger. Hence, it functions as a repository of all transactions. It also has a very high level of security.

A blockchain is composed of records known as blocks. Every new block that is added to the blockchain must first be verified and pass through a series of confirmations. This is to ensure that the record that is being added is legitimate and genuine. Once a record is added to the blockchain, it can no longer be removed, altered, or withdrawn. Every new block that is added is connected to the previous block using what is known as a hash pointer. This makes all the records or blocks on the blockchain to be interconnected with one another. No part of the blockchain can be amended, changed, removed, or in any way be modified, unless there is a concurrence of at least a majority (51%) of the users in the network. Take note that the blockchain is connected to a vast network of computers. As a distributed ledger, any changes or additions made to any of the records will be reflected to all other users. Hence, if a certain record is added, then such record will be distributed to all the other users in the network, and so they will also be informed about it.

The blockchain is public in the sense that all transactions are viewable and verifiable to everyone. Do not worry; as we have already discussed, all of your personal information remains confidential. The blockchain is also known for being decentralized, which means that there is no central authority or organization that exercises control over it. Therefore, you can rest assured that it is free from any and all forms of bias, manipulation, undue control, and advantage.

As we have already discussed, blockchain technology is highly secure. For an attack against the blockchain to be successful, it must possess at least 51% of the total hash rate of the entire network. Since the blockchain is spread over a vast computer network, obtaining the said 51% is virtually impossible.

Today, blockchain is gaining popularity of its own apart from it being associated with the use of cryptocurrencies. This is because blockchain technology can also be applied to things other than cryptocurrencies and financial-related matters. In fact, those who people who may not like cryptocurrencies are very much interested in exploring possible opportunities of using blockchain technology.

CHAPTER 5:
WALLETS AND HOW TO SECURELY STORE BITCOIN

Why do you need a bitcoin wallet? Well, before you can start using and investing in bitcoins, you first need to have a place where you can store bitcoins. The place where you keep or store your bitcoins is what is known as a bitcoin wallet. There are different kinds of bitcoin wallets that you can use. You should understand their differences so that you will know just which wallet type will best suit your needs. Here are the different types of bitcoin wallets:

• *Web Wallet*

A web wallet is also known as an *online wallet*. This is the most commonly used type of bitcoin hot wallet in the world. Good examples of a bitcoin web wallet are Coinbase, GreenAddress, and Exodus. A web wallet is very convenient to use. You simply have to connect to the Internet to manage your wallet account. Although there have been security issues with web wallets in the past, it is noteworthy that many web wallets have already upgraded their security features, which makes the possibility of being hacked extremely difficult, if not impossible. It is also very easy to make a web wallet. You simply have to sign up for an account with a wallet provider. The whole signing up process only takes less than three minutes to complete.

• *Mobile Wallet*

A bitcoin mobile wallet is another type of hot wallet. As the name implies, it is the kind of bitcoin wallet that you can download on your mobile phone. Many web wallets also function as a mobile wallet. Normally, you can download the mobile wallet as an application from the Apple and/or GooglePlay store. These days, it is very easy and convenient to just use your phone to access the Internet. A mobile wallet will allow you to manage your account, send and receive bitcoins, and even buy and sell bitcoins, simply by using your mobile device.

• *Desktop Wallet*

A bitcoin desktop wallet is a type of cold wallet. Hence, it has a greater security than the aforementioned hot wallets. When you use a desktop wallet, you will store your bitcoins in a computer. The computer does not necessarily have to be a desktop computer. A laptop computer will also work just fine. Keep in mind that unlike a hot wallet, a cold wallet is not exposed to the hazards of the Internet. Therefore, when you use a desktop wallet, you should not connect the computer to the Internet anymore in order to keep it secure and protected.

• *Hardware Wallet*

A hardware wallet is another type of bitcoin cold wallet. It is also like a desktop wallet, but instead of keeping your public and private keys in a computer, you store them in some form of hardware, such as a USB. There are now specialized wallets being sold in the market precisely for this purpose. One of the most popular and highly recommended hardware wallets is the *Ledger Nano*. Just like when using a desktop wallet, you should avoid connecting your hardware wallet to a computer that is connected to the Internet or a computer that is affected by a virus or any kind of malware. This is an important preventive measure to keep your hardware wallet safe and secure. Again, when it comes to using a cold wallet, the main priority is the security of your wallet account.

• *Paper Wallet*

A paper wallet is where you store and print your public and private keys on paper. This is a very popular kind of cold wallet. It is suggested that you print several copies just in case you lose a copy. Needless to say, you should store them in a safe place. It is also common for a paper wallet to have a QR code that you will need to scan before you can access your account and transfer funds. Simply put, you need to be in possession of the paper wallet in order to gain full access to your bitcoin wallet account.

Which Wallet Type Should You Use?

When deciding which type of bitcoin wallet to use, you have to consider how you intend to use bitcoins. If you intend to make regular transactions, then you should use a hot wallet. Most hot wallets are available on the web as well as on mobile; hence, as far as convenience is concerned, you can rest assured that you will not have a problem with it. However, if you just want to make a long-term investment in bitcoin and if you are concerned about the security of your wallet, then you can use a cold wallet. Of course, you are not limited to using just a single wallet. Hence, if you want, you can use both kinds of bitcoin wallets, depending on your needs and how you intend to use bitcoins. You can also use multiple hot wallets at the same time. As the saying goes, "Do not put all your eggs in one basket." The same advice applies when it comes to storing your bitcoins.

Tips to Securely Store your Bitcoins

Regardless of whether you are using a hot or cold wallet, the security of your bitcoin wallet remains of high importance. Here are the best practices that you should observe in order to keep your bitcoin wallet safe and secure:

- *Use a strong password.*

Be sure to use a strong password. A strong password should combine lower and uppercase letters. You should also use numbers and symbols. Needless to say, it should not be something that other people can guess correctly. Therefore, do not use your birthday or your alias as a password. It is also advised that you use a long password of at least 15 characters long. From time to time, you should also update (change) your password.

- *Request a new bitcoin wallet address.*

Most bitcoin wallets will allow you to request a new bitcoin wallet address at any time and as many times as you want. Do not worry; this is very easy to do and you do not have to pay anything. You can do this with just a few clicks of a mouse and in less than 10 seconds. Take note that a single bitcoin wallet can generate many different wallet addresses. It is the wallet address that is used when sending and receiving bitcoins. It is a good practice to request a new bitcoin wallet address for every new transaction that you make. This is an effective way to minimize the exposure of a certain bitcoin wallet address, which is a good preventive measure that can minimize your risk. Again, make it a habit to request and use a new bitcoin wallet address every time that you make a transaction.

- *Check if the page is secure.*

Before you input any sensitive information, like your account password, on a website, you should first see to it that the page is secure. This is easy to do. Simply look at the URL bar and you should see a green padlock and/or the word "Secure" somewhere on the side of the URL bar. This signifies that the page is secure and that it is safe to key in sensitive information. Keep in mind that you should never enter your password or any other sensitive information if you are not sure if the page is secure.

- *Avoid public Wi-Fi connections.*

These days, it is very easy to connect to public Wi-Fi, especially when you are not at home. Although it is okay to use public Wi-Fi, especially if you are just browsing websites, it is not recommended that you access your bitcoin wallet over a public connection. The reason is because there are hackers out there who take advantage of public Wi-Fi connections and use them to pry into other users connected to the public Wi-Fi. A public Wi-Fi is mostly unsecure by nature, so you should not use it if you are going to input any sensitive information or when accessing/managing your bitcoin wallet.

Some notes when using a cold wallet

When you are using a cold wallet, you should make sure that the cold wallet is of good quality. Keep in mind that although a cold wallet can protect you against hackers and all other related Internet risks, it cannot protect you from the risk of having your wallet stolen or broken. Hence, be sure that it is in a good working condition and keep it in a safe place.

(It is noteworthy that these practices are also as effective when you are storing altcoins.)

CHAPTER 6:
TOP 10 CRYPTOCURRENCIES AND WHERE TO TRACK THEM

To date, there are more than 1,000 cryptocurrencies in the market, but only a handful of them are able to draw enough market attention to establish a real value. Let us look at the top 10 cryptocurrencies in the market:

✓ Bitcoin (BTC)

Of course, the first one on the list should be *bitcoin*. Bitcoin is the leading standard when it comes to cryptocurrencies. Indeed, it is the most successful cryptocurrency in the world. As of January 19, 2018, the price of 1 bitcoin is around $11,572 USD.

✓ Ethereum (ETH)

Ethereum is considered by many as the second most successful cryptocurrency in the world. There are even some people who strongly believe that Ethereum will be able to overtake bitcoin and be the number one cryptocurrency in 2018. However, many experts say that this is far from happening, as bitcoin remains very strong in the market. Ethereum promotes the use of smart contracts and distributed applications on its blockchain. Ethereum is the platform, while its cryptocurrency token is known as *ether*. As of January 19, 2018, the price of 1 ether is around $1,058.

✓ Ripple (XRP)

Unlike most cryptocurrencies that seem to antagonize banks as if to take their place, Ripple actually helps banks. Ripple was launched in 2012, and it "enables banks to settle cross-border payments in real time, with end-to-end transparency, and at lower costs." Also, unlike other cryptocurrencies, Ripple is structured in such a way that it does not need mining. As of January 19, 2018, the price of Ripple is around $1.64 USD.

✓ Zcash (ZEC)

Zcash was introduced in the market in 2016. It is based on a decentralized and open-source system. Zcash defines itself as follows: "If Bitcoin is like http for money, Zcash is https." Zcash gives primary importance to privacy. It allows the use of selective transparency. This selective transparency allows its users to enjoy a high level of privacy by hiding the details as to the sender, recipient, and even the amount involved in a transaction. This is referred to as a "shielded transaction." As of January 19, 2018, the price of 1 Zcash is around $501.

✓ Dash (DASH)

Dash used to be known in the market as Darkcoin. Dash is structured in such a way that its transactions can be made to be almost untraceable. It was introduced in the market in 2014, and it was able to quickly establish a name for itself. Although its name changed from Darkcoin into Dash, its features remain the same. The term, Dash, is short for Digital Cash. As of January 19, 2018, the price of Dash is around $849.

✓ Litecoin (LTE)

Litecoin was released in 2011. Hence, it is not a new cryptocurrency player in the market. It is one of the early competitors of bitcoin. If bitcoin was considered gold, then Litecoin wanted to be the silver version. Its features closely resemble those of bitcoin. However, Litecoin has a faster block generation than bitcoin, and this means that it can confirm and complete transactions much faster than bitcoin. As Proof of Work (PoW), Litecoin uses what is known as "scrypt." As of January 19, 2018, the price of LTE is around $196.

✓ Monero (XMR)

Monero was made out of the donations coming from the cryptocurrency community. It was introduced in the market in 2014. Its main focus is on decentralization and scalability. It promotes the use of ring signatures. When you use ring signatures, a legitimate transaction gets mixed up with a set of false transactions. This is an effective way to "hide" or make your transactions private since people will not be able to identify the legitimate transactions from those that are false, especially that the false transactions will also appear and look as if they were valid. AS of January 19, 2018, the price of XMR is around $337.

✓ Lisk (LSK)

Lisk is quite a new cryptocurrency. It was introduced in the market in 2016. It functions like Ethereum in the sense that it allows the use of applications on its blockchain. When you use Lisk, you can create your blockchain on top of the Lisk blockchain. As of January 19, 2018, the price of Lisk is around $23.

OmiseGO (OMG)

OmiseGO was launched in 2017, which makes it a fairly new cryptocurrency. It aims to provide a simplified and more effective financial service. Its slogan is "Unbank the Banked." It is one of the altcoins in the market that is based on Ethereum blockchain. In 2017, the price of OMG increased by more than 1,200% in just a few weeks. As of January 19, 2018, the price of OMG is around $17 USD.

✓ NEO (NEO)

NEO is known as China's largest cryptocurrency. It was launched in 2014 under the name *Antshares*, but it was renamed later on to NEO by its developers. NEO is also the name by which this cryptocurrency is commonly known. People also call it as China's Ethereum. It functions just like Ethereum. NEO is China's first and number one coin. NEO has also seen a significant increase in price in recent months. As of January 19, 2018, the price of NEO is around $145.

Additional Notes:

The prices of these cryptocurrencies fluctuate continuously. You can easily track their prices by visiting the following sites:

https://coinmarketcap.com/
https://www.coingecko.com/en

CHAPTER 7:
MOST POPULAR CRYPTOCURRENCY EXCHANGES

If you do a search online, you will find many different cryptocurrency exchanges. As an investor, it is important that you work with a trustworthy and reliable exchange platform. Let us look at the most popular cryptocurrency exchanges:

✓ **Coinbase**

Coinbase has millions of investors and customers in the world. It is probably the most popular exchange platform in the world. Coinbase makes it very easy to buy and sell selected cryptocurrencies. Coinbase currently offers only three cryptocurrencies: Bitcoin, Ether, and Litecoin. Coinbase has an excellent reputation and is trusted by many professional investors.

✓ **Kraken**

Kraken started in 2011. It offers many types of cryptocurrencies, including Ripple, Monero, ICONOMI, and other altcoins. It does not just allow you to buy and sell cryptocurrencies, but you can also trade bitcoins with fiat money, such as the U.S. dollar, Japanese Yen, and others.

✓ **Cex.io**

Cex.io also provides different cryptocurrencies to choose from. Just like Kraken, it also allows you to trade cryptocurrencies with fiat money. It also offers a cold storage. It also provides a simple way to buy bitcoins at a price that is close to the actual market rate. This is excellent for traders and investors who are just starting out.

✓ Poloniex

Poloniex offers many cryptocurrency choices. It was launched in 2014, and is now one of the most popular cryptocurrency exchanges. Its trading environment looks professional and secure with more than 100 cryptocurrency pairs to choose from. It has a high trading volume. It is also fast and easy to create an account with Poloniex. You would not have a hard time with it even if you are a complete beginner. It also imposes a low fee for trading.

✓ Shapeshift

Shiftshift is one of those rare platforms where you do not even have to sign up for an account. You can trade directly using a direct and straightforward approach. It does not provide any policy for fiat money, but only offers the exchange between and among different cryptocurrencies. This is simplest and fastest way to convert one cryptocurrency into another.

✓ Bitstamp

Bitstamp is not a new platform. In fact, it has been in the market since 2011, and it is trusted by many cryptocurrency investors. It provides its users with high security features, such as two-factor authentication and multi-signature technology. Its customer support is also available round the clock. Indeed, it has earned a good reputation in the cryptocurrency community.

✓ Binance

Binance is another famous cryptocurrency exchange platform. It also has an excellent mobile application. Although it may not offer a professionally designed platform, you can be sure that trading with Binance makes the process really simple and easy. There are also various cryptocurrencies to choose from. The site is easy to use, and it is also recommended by many serious cryptocurrency investors.

✓ Bitfinex

This is considered as one of the largest cryptocurrency exchange in the market. Although it is trusted and used by many investors, Bitfinex already got hacked which resulted to the loss of around $72,000,000 worth of bitcoins. It has also faced several technical issues. Still, many cryptocurrency investors are happy and satisfied with Bitfinex.

CHAPTER 8:
INVESTMENT STRATEGIES

If you want to have continuous success in the cryptocurrency market, you need to apply effective and powerful strategies that can turn the odds in your favor and increase your chances of making a profit. Here are notable strategies that you should learn and practice:

• *Fundamental Analysis*

As they say, "Knowledge is power." When you use fundamental analysis, you need to have knowledge of the fundamentals or the basics. The key to using this strategy is to have as much knowledge and understanding of the cryptocurrency market, as well as the cryptocurrency that you intend to invest in. When you do fundamental analysis, you should make it a habit to be updated on the latest news, especially those that are closely related to the cryptocurrency market, such as news about the economy, market competition, market acceptance, technological developments, and related government regulations, among others. You need to gain as much information as possible. It is a basic rule in investing that the more that you understand the market, the more likely that you can come up with a profitable investment decision.

If you are serious about making money by investing in cryptocurrencies, then it is considered a must that you learn and use this strategy. To give you an idea: When Russia legalized the use of bitcoins in its jurisdiction, the price of bitcoin and other cryptocurrencies increased. However, when China declared that it would shut down its local exchanges, the price of bitcoin and many other altcoins dropped significantly. When it was featured on the news that the co-founder of bitcoin sold all his bitcoins and invested in bitcoin cash (an offshoot of bitcoin), the price of bitcoin fell and the price of bitcoin cash increased. As you can see, by simply gaining basic information and doing your analysis, you can have a good idea on how certain cryptocurrencies will respond in the market. Once you can predict how certain cryptocurrencies will most likely move in the market, you can then take appropriate actions to take advantage of the market and make a profit.

This strategy can be applied even if you are using a different strategy. In fact, this is so important that it has also been referred to as the lifeblood of investment. Whether investing in cryptocurrencies, stocks, bonds, or real estate, you will definitely find this strategy very helpful.

• *Technical Analysis*

If you are more of a visual person, then you will probably enjoy doing technical analysis. When you use this approach, you will have to study charts and graphs that show the price movements (past and present trends) of a cryptocurrency. The concept behind technical analysis is that all the many factors that influence a cryptocurrency have their final effect upon the price. Hence, by simply analyzing the price movements of a cryptocurrency, you also get to deal with all the many elements that affect it. In a way, this is like a simplified version of fundamental analysis.

When you use technical analysis, you need to learn how to read and identify patterns. Yes, patterns do exist from time to time. However, take note that they often come and go. Therefore, do not expect to always see a pattern or trend every time that you look at a certain chart or graph. A common mistake is to force yourself to see a pattern even if there is nothing at all to be seen. You need to keep an open mind. However, once you recognize a certain pattern, then you should be ready to take advantage of it.

Just like fundamental analysis, you can combine technical analysis with another strategy. In fact, many cryptocurrency investors combine both fundamental and technical analysis. According to experts, mastery of fundamental and technical analysis can increase your chances of success by more than 75%.

• *Averaging Down*

This is a good way to earn a high amount of profit. However, this is also an aggressive approach so you need to be cautious when you use it. The best way to explain this strategy is by using an example: Let us assume that you want to invest in bitcoin and that the price of bitcoin is $9,000. If the price of bitcoin increases, then you make an easy profit. However, if the price drops, for example, down to $8,700, then you should make a buy order at the said lower amount. Now, if it decreases again, say, down to $8,300, then you should make another buy order, and so on and so forth. Simply put, you just have to keep buying the cryptocurrency concerned while its price keeps on falling. Now, although this may seem like you are investing in a losing asset, the truth here is that you are actually making a profitable investment. The key to profit here is when the price of the cryptocurrency (in this case, bitcoin) involved recovers either back to its original value (its price when you first applied this strategy), or higher. When this happens, all the buy positions that you have made will experience a nice profit.

This strategy is also a good way to take advantage of the volatility of the market, especially when the prices of cryptocurrencies constantly rise and fall. Although this strategy may seem very practical and profitable, it is noteworthy that it is also highly aggressive, so you need to be careful with it.

• *Buy and hold*

This is probably the most basic strategy that you can use. However, it is worth noting that there are people who have earned millions of profit simply by using this strategy. So, how does it work? As the name implies, it involves buying a particular cryptocurrency and then holding on to it. You should hold on to it as you wait for its price to increase. Once its price increases over time, you can then sell it at a profit. How profitable is this strategy? Well, just imagine having invested in bitcoin four years ago using this strategy, then you would have made a very high profit by now. Although this strategy is often used for a long-term investment, you can also use this strategy for a short-term investment.

Before you apply this strategy, it is important for you to first study the cryptocurrency market. You need to identify the cryptocurrency that is most likely going to increase in price. You cannot just use this strategy at random. You also need to make sure that you are investing in a valuable and profitable cryptocurrency.

• *Altcoin Spread Out*

These days, many investors like to invest in altcoins. The reason is that altcoins, especially the new ones, have such a big room for improvement. In fact, it is not uncommon to find altcoins that increase their value by more than 200% in just a short period of time. When you use this strategy, you should divide your total capital into parts. There is no hard and fast rule as to how you should divide your capital, but it is suggested that you divide it into at least four equal parts. This will give you four chances or investments. If you divide it into four, then it means that you will invest in four altcoins. The key is to invest in a valuable altcoin whose price will most likely increase significantly. Pay attention to new and start-up altcoins in the market as they have a big room for growth and improvement. It is normal for start-up altcoins to increase even as high as 1,000% over time. Hence, even if you divide your capital into four and only one of those four investments turns out to be profitable, there is a good chance that you will still end up in positive profit. There are three points to consider when choosing a strong altcoin: value, effective promotion, and market acceptance. Make sure that you invest in an altcoin that has a good value. It should also be effectively promoted by its developers and its followers/supporters. Last but not least, it should attract the attention and interest of the market.

CONCLUSION

Thanks for making it through to the end of this book. We hope it was informative and able to provide you with all of the tools you need to achieve your goals whatever they may be.

The next step is to apply everything that you have learned and start earning continuous profits. It is time for you to put your knowledge into actual practice. *Now* is the perfect time for you to make a difference and change your life for the better.

Finally, if you found this book useful in anyway, a review on Amazon is always appreciated!

www.ingramcontent.com/pod-product-compliance
Lightning Source LLC
Chambersburg PA
CBHW070202230526
45471CB00002B/780